STONEHENGE

Published by Creative Education
123 South Broad Street
Mankato, Minnesota 56001

Creative Education is an imprint of The Creative Company.

Designed by Stephanie Blumenthal
Production design by The Design Lab
Art direction by Rita Marshall

Photographs by Corbis (James L. Amos, Archivo Iconografico, S.A., David Aubrey, Peter Beck, Bettmann, Hans Dieter Brandl; Frank Lane Picture Agency, Brooklyn Museum of Art, Andrew Brown; Ecoscene, Gary W. Carter, W. Cody, M. Dillon, Robert Estall, Werner Forman, David Gallant, Phillip Gould, Chinch Gryniewicz, Nick Hawkes; Ecoscene, Chris Hellier, Historical Picture Archive, Angelo Hornak, Jeremy Horner, Paul Hutley; Eye Ubiquitous, David Lees, George McCarthy, Gideon Mendel, Maurice Nimmo; Frank Lane Picture Agency, Alain Nogues, Richard T. Nowitz, PBNJ Productions, Carl & Ann Purcell, Roger Ressmeyer, Homer Sykes, Stapleton Collection, Sandro Vannini, David H. Wells, Randy Wells, Roger Wilmshurst; Frank Lane Picture Agency, Adam Woolfitt), Getty Images (Derke/O'Hara)

Printed in the United States of America

Library of Congress Cataloging-in-Publication Data
Shofner, Shawndra.
Stonehenge / by Shawndra Shofner.
p. cm. — (Ancient wonders of the world)
Includes index.
ISBN 1-58341-360-X
1. Stonehenge (England)—Juvenile literature. 2. Wiltshire (England)—Antiquities—Juvenile literature.
3. Megalithic monuments—England—Wiltshire—Juvenile literature I. Title. II. Series.

DA142.S53 2004   936.2'19—dc22   2004055268

First edition

2 4 6 8 9 7 5 3 1

Stonehenge

SHAWNDRA SHOFNER

CREATIVE ✺ EDUCATION

Although the formations at Stonehenge may look like simple rock structures, they are actually amazing feats of construction, the purpose of which no one has been able to determine with certainty.

On rolling farmland dotted with grazing cows and sheep, the ruins of a prehistoric stone monument rise from southern Britain's Salisbury Plain. For thousands of years, curious visitors and surveyors have tried to understand these massive stones. Long ago, people believed that giants and magic played a part in the structure's cre-ation. Pioneering researchers called it a Roman temple, primitive calendar, or heavenly observatory. Today, **archaeologists** and historians are able to answer more accurately who built this monument, when, and how. Still, one question may forever go unanswered: Why did ancient people build this structure we call Stonehenge?

4

PREHISTORIC BUILDERS

Stone axes and arrowheads (below) found at Stonehenge provide information about the area's earliest inhabitants.

More than 6,000 years ago, bands of prehistoric people roamed the European landscape, surviving by hunting wild animals and gathering plants for food. Axes, arrowheads, and knives carved from bone, flint, and stone served as their only weapons and tools. Because they rarely stayed in one place very long, these wandering hunters and gatherers lived in temporary campsites consisting of brush lean-tos or animal-skin tents.

Around 3100 B.C., the people who lived in modern-day Ireland, Scotland, Wales, and Britain started to understand the life cycles of native plants and began practicing an early form of farming. They cut down towering pines, cleared away brush, and created garden plots in which they planted wild grains and root crops. They gradually learned how to tame and herd wild cows, pigs, goats, sheep, and dogs. No longer did they need to travel long distances in search of food. They settled in permanent, flat-roofed shelters near the land they farmed. As their agricultural methods improved, these early farmers ended up with surplus yields. Eventually, they learned how to store the extra food, and fewer people died of starvation.

By about 2100 B.C., the tribes of south Britain's Salisbury Plain seem to have adopted new religious beliefs, perhaps influenced

6

Salisbury Plain is a 300-square-mile (780 sq km) chalk, or limestone, plateau in southern England. Its short grasses and open land gave rise to agriculture about 5,000 years ago.

The lives of many prehistoric people revolved around the daily rise and fall of the sun and moon. It is likely that the circular shapes of these heavenly bodies influenced the shape into which people constructed their monuments.

Agriculture freed extra workers to dig large, circular ditches (opposite) and allowed the Beaker Folk to trade for bronze ax and lance heads (below).

by traders from other regions. They stopped burying their dead in **communal** graves and started burying them singly with pottery, metal tools, and weapons. They marked these single graves with mounds called *tumuli*. Archaeologists named this culture "Beaker Folk," because the clay drinking vessels found in their graves are shaped like the beakers used by chemists.

Although the Beakers had no written language, they continued their success as farmers and traded their surplus food for bronze tools and weapons made in modern-day Ireland and other parts of Europe. The

Beaker population thrived, and soon there were more people than were needed to farm and trade. These extra people went to work on community projects, such as the construction of an enclosure of **bluestones** within a ditch circle on Salisbury Plain—the beginnings of Stonehenge—in which to hold important tribal meetings and religious rituals that may have focused on the sun, moon, and stars.

During the next 100 years, the wealthiest families ruled the land. The richest, most powerful leaders likely enlisted the work force needed for a new task: removing the bluestone enclosure and replacing it with gigantic blocks

Bluestone (below), a hard rock named for its bluish tint, was used for part of the construction of the mysterious structures at Stonehenge. Today, most of the stones have a weathered look after being exposed to the elements for thousands of years.

of **sarsen**. Perhaps these rulers thought the magnificent stones would better convey an image of power and authority at their tribal meeting site. Maybe they sought to make the structure more spectacular for the god or gods they worshipped. Whatever their reason, the project required hundreds of workers and took nearly 200 years.

For reasons unknown, the Beaker population near Stonehenge suddenly declined around 1500 B.C. It is possible that the soil had become less fertile because the farmers planted the same grains in it year after year. Some farmers and their families

may have relocated. Farmers who remained probably took workers away from community projects and put them to work fertilizing the land with manure and cultivating different grains and roots. No structural improvements were made to Stonehenge, no new monuments were built nearby, and fewer cemeteries were added to the surrounding grounds. Even so, people must have continued to use Stonehenge for the next 400 years, because a long approach, or avenue, was added to it around 1100 B.C. Some time after that, Stonehenge was abandoned and not given serious attention for more than 3,000 years.

Much like farmers today, the ancient people of Salisbury Plain had to fertilize their fields (bottom) in order to increase grain production (top). Some people have suggested that Stonehenge may have functioned as a calendar to help ancient farmers determine planting and harvest times.

MEGALITHIC MONUMENT

More than 300 burial mounds lie within the 6,400 acres (2,600 ha) of the Stonehenge World Heritage Site.

The gigantic rock monument known as Stonehenge is more than 3,500 years old. Today, only part of the original monument remains on a landscape scattered with burial grounds two miles (3.2 km) west of the town of Amesbury, in England's southwestern county of Wiltshire. Time, gravity, erosion, pollution, and human intrusion have all contributed to fallen, broken, and missing stones. Yet even in its ruinous state, this **megalithic** monument that took thousands of prehistoric people more than 20 centuries to develop continues to command attention and strike awe.

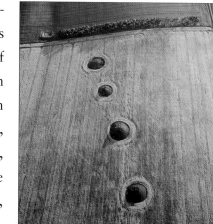

The circular ditch, or henge, surrounding the stones is about 330 feet (100 m) in diameter. Now filled in from thousands of years of weathering, it was the first development at the Stonehenge site. Using deer antler pickaxes and shovels fashioned from the shoulder blades of cows, it probably took about 175 men three weeks to dig its original depth of six feet (1.8 m). The interior bank initially stood about six feet (1.8 m) high but today appears as a low mound. Workers left at least two entrances, the main one pointing northeast in the direction of the midsummer sunrise. About 16.5 feet (5 m) inside the interior

In the 17th and 18th centuries, some surveyors thought the ancient people who built Stonehenge were not sophisticated enough to transport the large sarsen stones to the monument. They believed instead that the builders mixed up a sand-based composition similar to cement, poured it into molds, and created the huge blocks on site.

bank, the indentations of 56 evenly spaced pits form a barely visible ring. These pits (named Aubrey Holes after 17th-century English **antiquary** John Aubrey, who discovered them in 1666) probably held wood posts, but any such remains have long since decomposed.

About 1,000 years after the ditch was dug, workers widened its northeast entrance and created a distinct walkway to it that was bordered by a set of parallel ditches. Laborers then trekked 240 miles (385 km) northwest to the Preseli Mountains—a walk that took at least 10

days—and brought back about 80 bluestones, **igneous** gray rocks averaging 6.5 feet (2 m) tall and weighing about 4.4 tons (4 t) each.

Given the great effort that went into hauling them, the distant bluestones must have had some significant meaning to these ancient people. Crews probably placed the bluestone blocks on a **sledge** and pulled it with a leather or animal-hair rope across timber rollers to the coast. From there, people rafted them to land near the henge. Laborers framed the henge's northeast entrance with two bluestones. At the henge's center, they

The bluestones used in the construction of Stonehenge came from a quarry (left) in the Preseli Mountains of Wales. Rising 1,760 feet (535 m), these mountains are the only place in the British Isles where bluestones can be found.

The builders of Stonehenge were capable of fine timberwork and were able to shape logs (right) into rollers to move the huge stones used in the construction of the monument. As they worked, the builders probably heard the haunting cries of the stone curlew (below), which nests on the open ground of Salisbury Plain.

arranged bluestones in a double U-shape that opened to the northeast.

The most extraordinary change to Stonehenge took place around 2000 B.C. Laborers dismantled the bluestone arrangement and replaced it with 44-ton (40 t) sarsen blocks. It probably took about 600 workers to manage a sledge carrying just one of these enormous stones. Using timber rollers, they hauled the blocks 20 miles (30 km) to Stonehenge from Marlborough Downs, a region of hills and valleys to the north. Using an ingenious combination of manpower, levers, ramps, and ropes, workers

erected a horseshoe shape of 5 **trilithons** by raising 10 of the largest sarsen blocks—some up to 24 feet (7.3 m) tall—and topping every two with one sarsen **lintel**. Around the outside of the trilithon horseshoe, crews set up a circle of 30 sarsen stones and topped them with a continuous ring of lintels. This circle stood about 16.5 feet (5 m) tall.

By around 1550 B.C., after rearranging the bluestones several more times, laborers placed them in their final setting: a short circle just inside the sarsen circle and a smaller horseshoe just inside the sarsen horseshoe. Of the original monument, only 25 sarsens and 18 bluestones stand upright today.

Builders used a classic woodworking method to keep the massive lintels in place on top of Stonehenge's upright sarsens. They carved indentations on the underside of the lintel stones that fit precisely into pegs on top of the uprights. They also shaped the lintels with tongue-and-groove joints so that they locked together edge to edge.

PAST, PRESENT, AND FUTURE

One of Stonehenge's great trilithons toppled in 1797, probably because gypsies and other wanderers often sought shelter at the site and dug pits near the base of the trilithon in which to build fires for cooking. The loosened ground no longer supported the heavy stones.

The tranquil beauty of the site inspired American William Trost Richards to paint Stonehenge *(opposite) around 1882.*

Stonehenge has beckoned people for thousands of years, sometimes to its detriment. In the Middle Ages, people who lived nearby chipped blocks off the stones and used them for their own building purposes. In recent centuries, visitors used hammers to chisel away souvenirs. Over the years, religious fanatics, believing Stonehenge was a place for devil worship, have tried to destroy it. As recently as 100 years ago, farmers broke chunks off of the magnificent stones and used them as fill for roads.

Many people took great care in studying the monument, however, and documented some great discoveries. William Stukeley, an English antiquary and scholar of sacred history, mapped the surrounding landscape and noted in 1721 that the arrangement of the stones aligned with positions of the sun and moon. English archaeologists William Cunnington and Sir Richard Colt Hoare uncovered pots from the **Bronze Age** in the early 1800s. Many of Cunnington and Hoare's excavations also involved returning fallen or leaning stones to their original upright position.

American astronomer Gerald S. Hawkins not only agreed with Stukeley's assertion that the monument aligned with the sun, moon, and stars, but he also

Farmlands near Stonehenge became a worldwide spectacle in the 1970s when flattened circles of various sizes mysteriously appeared in wheat and oat fields. In 1991, two British artists—Doug Bower and Dave Chorley—admitted to being crop circle creators, diffusing the popular myth that the circles were made by aliens.

A snowflake-shaped crop circle was one of many to appear on Salisbury Plain in the last four decades.

claimed that it predicted their movements across the sky and that the placement of the Aubrey Holes was linked to lunar eclipses. Hawkins's ideas gave rise to the new field of **archaeoastronomy**. In the 1940s and '50s, English archaeologist Richard Atkinson dated the phases of Stonehenge's construction. Archaeologists today use methods such as **radiocarbon dating** and **magnetometry** to learn

more about Stonehenge. Still, no amount of technology can reveal with any certainty why it was built.

Ever since Stonehenge was rediscovered in the 1400s, people have been telling stories to explain it. Up until the 1600s, many people believed that giants, gods, or wizards set the stones in place. In the 1700s, people thought the stones were enchanted. Some people rubbed their wounds over the rocks to heal them; others chipped pieces from the monument and dropped them into their wells to get rid of toads and snakes. Still others collected water they poured over the stones because they believed the water became charged with medicinal powers. Even today, some people say that the spaces between the stones are gateways to other dimensions of time, or that the whole structure is a landing site for aliens.

Many Druids today regard Stonehenge as a temple and gather there for a ceremony to celebrate the longest day of the year. Dressed in their ritual robes, they arrive at the site in the middle of the night in order to be ready to witness the early morning sunrise.

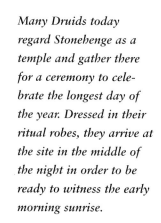

Without nearby trees against which to compare Stonehenge, it can be hard to judge the monument's size until standing next to one of its massive stones.

In the late 1970s, large numbers of visitors flocking to Stonehenge on foot caused land erosion near the stones. Fearing the stones might topple over, custodians surrounded the entire monument with a fence. In 1986, the United Nations Educational, Scientific, and Cultural Organization (UNESCO) made Stonehenge and the surrounding area a protected World Heritage Site because of its archaeological and cultural importance. Today, Stonehenge attracts nearly one million visitors a year.

Plans are underway to return the setting of Stonehenge to the way it looked 3,000 years ago. The British government intends to construct tunnels in place of two highways—one that passes within 550 feet (168 m) of Stonehenge's southern edge, and another that accesses a parking lot and outdated visitor facility to the north. A new interpretive center will be built about two and a half miles (4 km) away, complete with ample parking, two theaters, a food court, and a souvenir shop.

These plans have given many lovers of history hope that a pastoral countryside similar to that of ancient times will soon surround Stonehenge once again. Visitors will again be greeted by a green, serene landscape complete with blooming orchids and fluttering butterflies as they travel back in time to see perhaps the most famous prehistoric monument in the world.

The great bustard, a bird as tall as a deer and weighing up to 45 pounds (20 kg), will soon inhabit the grasslands around Stonehenge as it did years ago. Thirty young birds were brought in from Saratov, Russia, in 2004 to replace the native population that was wiped out by hunting 150 years ago.

The great bustard (bottom left) will soon rejoin swallowtail butterflies (bottom right) and vibrant orchids (top right) on the treeless grasslands (top left) of Salisbury Plain.

SEEING THE WONDER

Although Stonehenge is not the largest stone circle in the world, it is one of the most impressive, as it is the only one topped with lintels. While tourists used to be able to explore the monument from among the stones, today it is protected by a fence.

Europe features many historic sites that draw the eager tourist, but few are as old or as spellbinding as Stonehenge. The closest major city to Stonehenge is London, England. Many visitors embark on a 90-minute train ride from London's Waterloo Station to the town of Salisbury. They then board a bus for a 40-minute ride from Salisbury to Stonehenge (buses leave Salisbury for the prehistoric monument every hour or so).

Other visitors get to Stonehenge by way of the nearby town of Amesbury. From Amesbury, tourists can either walk two miles (3.2 km) to Stonehenge, catch a bus, or take a taxi. A unique but more expensive way to visit the site is from the sky; helicopter flights from Amesbury lasting half an hour are available as well.

As of 2005, admission costs at Stonehenge are about $8 for adults and $4 for children. Visitors can follow a walkway around the monument while listening to a self-guided audio tour. A protective fence surrounds the monument,

Whether reached by train, taxi, or bus, alone or with a group, a trip to the mysterious Stonehenge is sure to leave the tourist with a sense of awe and wonder. It was obviously an important site for its ancient builders, who devoted an estimated 30 million hours of labor to its construction.

In 1999, a British archaeologist discovered a large, stern face carved into the side of one of the standing sarsen stones. Four years later, lasers revealed carvings of ax heads up to 3,800 years old.

Located in an area of England that is steeped in history, myth, and legend, Stonehenge may never reveal all of its secrets.

but private access to the inner circle of stones can be arranged in advance (to see more details, visit the Web site www.english-heritage.org.uk/stonehenge).

The weather at Stonehenge can be damp any time of the year, so warm clothing and footwear, as well as a raincoat and umbrella, are necessities. Southern Britain's rainy season runs from October to January, but the temperatures rarely fall below freezing due to the relatively warm air that blows in from the nearby sea.

In the summer, temperatures average a cool 64 °F (18 °C).

As is the case with any trip abroad, foreign travelers need to be sure their **passport** is current before leaving for Britain. Visitors who want to see not only Stonehenge but other popular tourist spots in England may consider purchasing the Great British Heritage Pass, a prepaid card that allows free or discounted entry to more than 600 sites in Britain.

STONE  HENGE

QUICK FACTS

Location: Southern Britain; 80 miles (129 km) south of London on Salisbury Plain

Age: ~ 5,000 years

Composition: Bluestone and sarsen (sandstone)

Years to complete: ~ 2,000 (about 3100–1100 B.C.)

Architects/builders: Prehistoric farmers and Beakers

Key physical dimensions:

Bank and ditch: 330 feet (100 m) in diameter

Aubrey Holes: 56 pits, each 3 feet (91 cm) wide and deep

Bluestones: Originally 80 stones averaging
6.5 feet (2 m) tall, weighing 4.4 tons (4 t) each

Sarsen circle: 100 feet (30 m) in diameter; 16 feet (5 m) tall

Trilithon sarsens: 24 feet (7.3 m) tall, each stone
weighing an average of 44 tons (40 t)

Annual visitors: ~ 1 million

Geographic setting: Grassland

Native plant life: Includes whitlow grass, red fescue grass, crested hair
grass, juniper shrubs, tuberous thistles, wild thyme, and moss

Native animal life: Includes chalkhill blue butterflies, stone curlew birds,
great crested newts, scarce forrester moths, and tawney bumblebees

antiquary—a person who collects and studies objects left by ancient people

archaeoastronomy—the study of ancient people and their relationship with the sun, moon, and stars as reflected in the monuments they built

archaeologists—scientists who learn about the past by digging up and studying old structures or objects

bluestones—blotchy, gray-brown rocks formed by volcanic activity

Bronze Age—the era (ranging from 3500 to 1000 B.C.) in which humans used bronze tools and weapons

communal—referring to something shared by many people

igneous—a type of rock made when volcanic lava cools and solidifies

lintel—a block of stone that sits horizontally across upright stones

magnetometry—a method of searching for underground artifacts using an instrument that senses the magnetic waves of buried metal

megalithic—referring to stone monuments constructed by primitive people

passport—a government-issued document that allows travelers to enter countries other than their own

radiocarbon dating—a scientific calculation that determines the age of an object based on its rate of decay

sarsen—a hard, fine-grained rock called sandstone; also a block of such rock

sledge—a wooden sled pulled across timber rollers to transport heavy objects such as sarsen stones

trilithons—a combination of three stones: two set upright and capped with the third

INDEX